Romans, Saxons & Vikings

The Wars of the Vikings

Martyn Whittock

KU-685-437

Heinemann

First published in Great Britain by
Heinemann Library
Halley Court, Jordan Hill, Oxford OX2 8EJ

a division of Reed Educational and Professional
Publishing Ltd

OXFORD FLORENCE PRAGUE MADRID
ATHENS MELBOURNE AUCKLAND
KUALA LUMPUR SINGAPORE TOKYO IBADAN
NAIROBI KAMPALA JOHANNESBURG
GABORONE PORTSMOUTH NH (USA)
CHICAGO MEXICO CITY SAO PAULO

Designed by Ken Vail Graphic Design, Cambridge

Illustrations by Andrew Sharpe

Printed in the UK by Jarrold Book Printing Ltd,
Thetford

00 99 98 97 96

10 9 8 7 6 5 4 3 2 1

ISBN 0 431 05974 8

British Library Cataloguing in Publication Data

Whittock, Martyn J. (Martyn John)
Wars of the Vikings
1. Vikings – Juvenile literature 2. Scandinavia –
History –
Juvenile literature
I. Title
948'.022

**For Hannah and Esther Whittock, fellow
explorers of Athelney – a reminder of the stories
of King Alfred, with love from Daddy.**

Acknowledgements

The Publishers would like to thank
the following for permission to
reproduce photographs.

Antikvarisk-Topografiska Arkivet: p.5,
p.27; Lesley and Roy Adkins: p.19;
Ashmolean Museum: p.17; British
Museum: p.8; Corpus Christi College,
Cambridge: p.15; English Heritage
Photographic Library: p.11; Michael
Holford: p.28; Royal Library,
Stockholm: p.25; University Museum
of National Antiquities, Oslo: p.7, p.13;
York Archaeological Trust: p.21, p.23

Our thanks also to Osprey Military
for the illustration on p.6

Cover photograph reproduced with
permission of C. M. Dixon.

Our thanks to Keith Stringer, of the
Department of History at Lancaster
University, for his comments in the
preparation of this book.

We should like to thank the following
schools for valuable comments made
regarding the content and layout of
this series: Fitzmaurice Primary School,
Bradford-on-Avon, Wiltshire; Tyersal
First School, Bradford, Yorkshire.

Details of written sources

M. Alexander, *The Earliest English
Poems*, Penguin 1977: 11A

J. Campbell (ed), *The Anglo-Saxons*,
Phaidon 1982: 9A

G. Garmonsway, *The Anglo-Saxon
Chronicle*, Dent 1972: 1B; 4A; 11B

I. Heath, A. McBride, *The Vikings*,
Osprey 1985: 2A; 2B; 3A; 4C; 10B; 13A

M. Magnusson, *Vikings*, BCA 1980:
1D; 12A; 12B; 13A

M. Wood, *In Search of the Dark Ages*,
BBC 1981: 9B; 10A

Contents

Clues from the Viking wars

The Vikings first attacked Anglo-Saxon England in AD789, when they arrived off the Dorset coast. This was the first of their raids. They went on to make many attacks on England and they conquered large parts of the country.

Three hundred years of war

For nearly 300 years Viking and **Anglo-Saxon** rulers fought each other. They fought for the right to control England. This lasted until AD1075.

Wars across Europe

England was not the only country invaded by the Vikings. Viking armies attacked Wales, Ireland and Scotland too. The Vikings attacked many other countries in Europe. They sailed to places as far apart as Iceland, Russia and Greece.

Evidence from the Viking war

Many different kinds of clues survive from the Viking wars. Some are shown here. But we have to be very careful how we use this evidence. For example, sometimes it only tells one side of the story. Sometimes it was written long after the events described and may not be true. Sometimes historians disagree about what the clues mean.

Source A

He rushed forward ahead of his troops hacking with both hands. Neither helmet, nor **armour** could stand against him. And everyone in his way fell back before him.

*This is a description of the Viking **King** Harald Hardrada in battle, at Stamford Bridge in AD1066. It comes from a story about this king's life. This is called 'King Harald's Saga'. But sagas were not written until the thirteenth century. This was 200 years after the battle, so we do not know if this was really what the battle was like.*

Source B

In this year Ethelfled, the 'Lady of the Mercians', captured the town called Derby with God's help. Four of her **thegns**, who were dear to her, were killed there inside the gates.

The Anglo-Saxon Chronicle for the year AD917 tells about an Anglo-Saxon leader, Ethelfled. The Chronicle gives us information about the wars with the Vikings, but it was written by the Anglo-Saxons. It only tells their side of the story.

Source D

Bitter is the wind tonight,
White the waves of the sea;
I have no fear the Viking hordes
Will sail the seas on such a night.

This is from an Irish poem from the ninth century. We do not know if we can always trust poems. They may have made Viking attacks sound worse than they were to make a better poem.

Source C

This picture of a Swedish Viking dates from the seventh century, the century before the Vikings started attacking England.

Evidence like this has made many people think that Vikings fought in helmets decorated with horns and wings. But no helmets decorated like this have ever been found anywhere.

Viking weapons

The Vikings were skilful fighters. They were skilled at making and using different kinds of weapons.

Different Viking weapons

The picture on this page shows a modern drawing of the weapons used by Vikings. These Vikings carry swords and an axe and a spear. They wear metal helmets and carry shields. One is protected by a **chainmail** shirt. This was made from rings of metal fixed together.

This is a modern artist's picture of a Viking attack. The artist used evidence like Source A to draw this.

Source A

These are real Viking weapons, from Norway. They were made in the ninth and tenth centuries.

Source B

They left their armour behind and went ashore with only their shields, helmets and spears. They wore their swords. Some also had bows and arrows.

This is a description of a Viking army in Yorkshire, in AD1066. It was written in 'King Harald's Saga', in the thirteenth century.

How do we know?

Source A shows that some Vikings did wear metal helmets. They carried wooden shields. It also shows that their weapons included swords, spears and axes. The wooden parts of the spears and axes have rotted away, but the metal spearpoints and axe heads have been found.

Source B shows that Vikings in England used some of these weapons. They had shields, helmets, spears and swords. Some of them had **armour**. This was probably chainmail. But this source shows that some had bows and arrows too.

How did the Vikings fight?

The Vikings fought battles both on the land and at sea. They used different ways to try to defeat their enemies.

The shield wall

Viking **warriors** carried shields. These protected them from the weapons of their enemies. In battle the Vikings stood side by side, with their shields in front. Sometimes the shields overlapped. This made it hard for their enemies to break through and kill them.

The swine wedge

Two warriors stood at the front. Three other warriors stood behind them. Five more stood behind them, to make a **wedge**. These warriors pushed into the enemy army.

Fighting at sea

Most Viking battles were fought on land but some were fought at sea. In a sea battle, Vikings tied their boats together to make a **raft**. The biggest ship was in the middle. Warriors tried to climb on board the enemy ships.

Source A

They rushed forward without armour. They were as mad as dogs, or wolves. They bit their shields and were as strong as bears, or wild boars. They killed people with one blow. Neither fire, nor iron could hurt them. This was the berserk fury.

This description of berserkers is from the 'Ynglinga Saga'. It was written in the thirteenth century.

Source B

A twelfth-century carving of a berserker.

8

It was their habit, if they were with their friends when they felt the berserk fury coming on, to go ashore. There they wrestled with large stones, or trees. Otherwise they were so angry they would have killed their friends.

This is from a thirteenth century story of how all twelve sons of one Viking warrior were berserkers.

The berserkers

Although Vikings sometimes rode captured horses to battle, they preferred to fight on foot. They would break through the enemy shield wall to get at and kill their enemies.

The most terrifying Viking warriors were 'berserkers'. They fought wildly and they often wore no **armour**. Sometimes they were so angry they bit their shields and howled like wild animals. Sometimes they wore the skins of wild animals. The word berserker means 'bear shirt'.

Some wore wolf skins and were called 'wolfcoats'. Some berserkers may have been mentally ill, or taken drugs.

How do we know?

Source A shows that some Viking warriors were wild. They bit their shields and fought like animals. Source B shows a warrior like this biting his shield in anger.

Source C shows how wild berserkers were. They may have been mentally ill. They were dangerous even to their friends.

The first Viking raids

The first Viking raid on England that we know about happened in AD789. In that year, three ships landed at Portland in Dorset, in the Anglo-Saxon kingdom of Wessex. Nearby, in Dorchester, lived a servant of the king of Wessex. He rode to Portland to see the visitors. The Vikings killed him. These first Vikings came from Norway.

Who were the raiders?

The **Anglo-Saxons** often called the raiders 'Danes', even though not all came from Denmark. They also called them 'Northmen' and **pagans**. A pagan is a person who is not a Christian. The raiders called themselves 'Vikings'. This word probably meant pirates who hid in secret places on the coast.

The attack on Lindisfarne

In AD793, Vikings attacked the famous Anglo-Saxon **monastery** at Lindisfarne (Holy Island), in the kingdom of Northumbria. The destruction of this church shocked and frightened people across England. They remembered it for a long time.

Source A

In those days there came for the first time three ships of Northmen from Horthaland. Then the **reeve** rode there and tried to make them go to the royal **manor**. For he did not know who they were. Then they killed him. These were the first ships of the Danes to come to England.

The Anglo-Saxon Chronicle for the year AD789 describes a Viking raid on Dorset. Horthaland is in Norway.

Kingdom of Northumbria

Lindisfarne

The first Viking raids.

Kingdom of Wessex

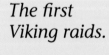
Portland

Source B

This gravestone from Lindisfarne may show Viking warriors. They are armed with swords and axes like those used by Vikings. It was probably carved some time after the attack.

Source C

Never before has such terror appeared in Britain, as we have now suffered from a pagan people. Nor was it thought possible that such an attack could come from the sea. See, the church of St Cuthbert, splashed with the blood of the priests of God. Its ornaments have been stolen.

A church leader, named Alcuin, wrote about the attack on Lindisfarne. Alcuin lived at the time of the attack, in AD793.

How do we know?

Source A shows that the Anglo-Saxons often mixed up the names they used for Vikings. In this source the Vikings are called Danes, even though they actually came from Norway.

Source C shows that the Viking attack on Lindisfarne shocked Anglo-Saxon people. Source B probably shows that people remembered the raid and recorded it on stone. But we cannot be sure that the **warriors** on the stone are really Vikings. It also shows that the church was not totally destroyed. People went on using it afterwards.

The 'Great Armies'

The great Viking attacks on England happened after AD835. The earlier attacks had been by Norwegians. Later, most warriors came from Denmark.

Attacks on western Europe

In AD834 Vikings attacked the **trading** town of Dorestadt. This is in the modern Netherlands. In AD835 they attacked the island of Sheppey, in the River Thames. For fifteen years they attacked places on both sides of the English Channel. Ireland was also attacked. Most attacks took place during the summer.

In AD850 Danish Vikings spent the winter in England. This showed Vikings could take over parts of **Anglo-Saxon** England. They were not just raiding and then going quickly home again.

The 'Great Army'

In AD865 a large Viking army spent the winter in East Anglia. The Anglo-Saxons called them 'micel here'. This means 'Great Army'. They were led by Halfdan, Ivar the Boneless and Ubbi. The East Anglians gave them horses to make them leave. They rode north to attack Northumbria.

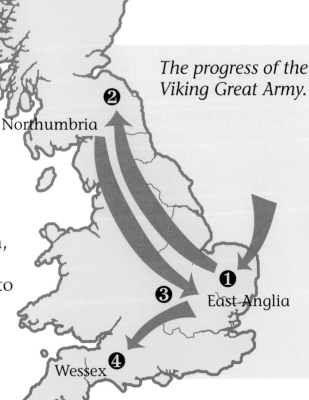

The progress of the Viking Great Army.

Northumbria

East Anglia

Wessex

Source B

A reconstruction of a Viking tapestry. It was buried with a ship at Oseberg, in Norway. It was made in about AD850.

The capture of York

The Great Army captured York in AD866. The Northumbrians were quarrelling amongst themselves. The Vikings killed two of their **kings**. In AD870 these Vikings returned to East Anglia. They killed its Anglo-Saxon king and seized the kingdom.

The 'Great Summer Army'

In AD871, a new Viking army arrived. It was led by Guthrum. Together with Vikings already in England, they attacked the Anglo-Saxon kingdom of Wessex.

How do we know?

The Vikings are usually thought of as sailors. But Source A shows that they would also ride horses when they needed to. These were given to them by Anglo-Saxons in East Anglia, to make them go away!

Source B shows that horses were important to Vikings. They rode on them and used them to pull loads.

King Alfred of Wessex – escape from disaster!

From AD871 the Vikings attacked the Anglo-Saxon kingdom of Wessex. In that year Wessex had a new king. He was named Alfred. Later people called him 'Alfred the Great'.

The attack on Alfred

In AD876 the Vikings, led by Guthrum, invaded Wessex. They finally left when Alfred gave them money.

Shortly after Christmas, in the first days of AD878, the Vikings returned! They almost captured Alfred. He was feasting with his closest friends and **warriors** at Chippenham, in Wiltshire.

The island of Athelney

Alfred was forced to run from the Vikings. He went into the marshes of Somerset, where he was safe from attack. Around Easter he built a fort there, on an island called Athelney. From there he planned his own attack on the Vikings.

Source A

In this year the **host** went secretly in midwinter after Twelfth Night to Chippenham. They rode over Wessex and captured it. Most people gave in to them, except Alfred the **king**. He and a few companions went with difficulties through woods and into secret places in the marshes.

From the Anglo-Saxon Chronicle, AD878.

Source B

After Easter, King Alfred, with a few men, made a fortress at a place called Athelney. And from it, with the **thegns** of Somerset, he struck out against the Danes.

This is from an account of Alfred's life, written by his friend, Bishop Asser, in the late ninth century.

Source C

*The treaty between Alfred and Guthrum. It is written in **Old English** – Alfred's language. This is a copy made in about AD1100.*

How do we know?

Source A shows that Alfred escaped from the Vikings with only a few followers. Source B tells us that they built a fort at Athelney. From there Alfred attacked Guthrum.

Source C shows us that Alfred and Guthrum made a treaty This ended the war between them.

Alfred fights back

Seven weeks after Easter, Alfred left Athelney. He travelled to eastern Somerset, where warriors loyal to him were waiting. Two days later he defeated the Viking army at the Battle of Edington, in Wiltshire. Guthrum was forced to surrender. A few weeks later Guthrum was baptized as a Christian. His Viking army returned to East Anglia. Wessex had survived.

In AD886 Guthrum agreed a **treaty** with Alfred. This promised peace between them. It also fixed a **border** between the land ruled by Alfred and by Guthrum.

Alfred starts to make Wessex stronger

Alfred survived the Viking attack on Wessex in AD878. He went on to increase the power of Wessex. He wanted to make it better prepared for fighting against the Vikings.

Alfred captures London

In AD886 Alfred captured London. He may have taken it from the Vikings, or he may have taken it from other **Anglo-Saxons**, who were friendly with the Vikings. He gave the city to a man named Ethelred. Ethelred ruled the parts of Mercia which the Vikings did not control. He married Alfred's daughter, Ethelfled.

The capture of London made Wessex stronger. It increased the land under Alfred's control. He was trying to make himself **king** of all the Anglo-Saxons. London was also a good place to **trade**.

Alfred and education

Most people who could read were monks and nuns. But the Vikings had destroyed many **monasteries** where the monks and nuns lived. This meant that fewer people could read. Even many powerful people in Wessex could not read.

Source A

I will send a copy to each **bishop** in my kingdom. And with each copy there will be an expensive pointer worth fifty **mancuses**.

*Alfred was writing about a book he translated from **Latin** into **Old English**. The book was worth fifty cows!*

16

Source B

This Anglo-Saxon jewel was found in AD1693, four miles from Alfred's fort at Athelney, in Somerset. The words say 'Alfred ordered me to be made'. It may be one of the book pointers mentioned by Alfred. A piece of wood may have been put in one end of it, to use as a pointer.

How do we know?

Source A shows that Alfred thought it was important that people across Wessex should read the books he had written in Old English. This was part of his plan to rebuild Wessex.

Source B is probably one of the pointers sent with one of these books, but we cannot be absolutely sure. It might have been made for another Anglo-Saxon named Alfred. But it was made at the time of King Alfred, and it would have cost a lot!

Alfred wanted to improve education. He believed people should know their Bibles and be good Christians. Then God would defend them from the Vikings. Also, he needed people who could read to carry out his orders. He encouraged clever people to **translate** good books into Old English, the language of the Anglo-Saxons. He did some of this translation work himself.

He sent these books to the bishops in Wessex. He sent expensive pointers with each book. These were to help people follow the words as they read.

17

Keeping the Vikings out

King Alfred tried to make it hard for Viking armies to attack Wessex in the future.

The burhs

Alfred ordered the building of forts across Wessex. Some were made by putting walls around old towns. Some forts were built for the first time. The forts were called **burhs**. People would be safe behind their walls. They were also places where people could **trade**. Alfred may have got this idea from forts built by earlier **Anglo-Saxon kings** in Mercia.

New ships

Alfred was not the first Anglo-Saxon king to build fighting ships, but he tried to make bigger and better ones. He may have copied ideas used in France to try to beat off Viking attacks. Alfred's new ships were very large. They needed 60 people to row them. The first time they were used they had problems, but later they had more success against Vikings.

Source A

Alfred ordered warships to be built. They were almost twice as long as before, some had sixty oars and some had more. They were not built like the Danes and Frisians made their ships. Instead, they were made the way that he thought was best.

From the Anglo-Saxon Chronicle, AD896. Frisians live on the coast of The Netherlands and north-west Germany. In Alfred's time they were famous sailors.

Source B

The king divided his army into two parts. This was so that there was always half at home and half out fighting. Other men had the duty of guarding the forts.

From the Anglo-Saxon Chronicle, AD893.

Source C

The earth walls of the Anglo-Saxon burh at Wareham, Dorset.

The fyrd

The army of Wessex was called the 'fyrd'. Alfred divided this army into two parts. Half were ready to fight. The other half could go home and look after their land. The new army also used horses to ride after Viking raiders.

How do we know?

Source A shows that Alfred tried to make better kinds of ships. He used his own ideas about how they should be built.

Sources B and C show his new ideas on land. Source B shows that Alfred made changes to his army. It also shows that soldiers guarded forts against the Vikings. Source C shows the earth walls of one of these forts.

We must be careful, though. The Anglo-Saxon Chronicle was written by people who supported Alfred. They wanted to make it sound as if all the best ideas were his. They did not mention other people who may have had these ideas before Alfred.

Fighting to rule the Danelaw

After King Alfred died in AD899, other kings of Wessex fought the Vikings. They fought about who would rule the Danelaw. This was the part of England ruled by Viking kings.

The wars of Edward the Elder and Ethelfled

Edward was the eldest son of **King** Alfred. He made everyone who lived south of the River Humber obey him. These were **Anglo-Saxons** and Danish Vikings. Edward was helped by his sister, Ethelfled. She had married Ethelred of Mercia and was called the 'Lady of the Mercians'. She built **burhs** across Mercia. She made friends with Vikings from Ireland. They agreed to fight the Viking kings of Northumbria for her. They hoped to win more riches for themselves.

Not all Anglo-Saxons liked King Edward. Some preferred Vikings. Edward's own cousin worked with the Vikings against him. Many Anglo-Saxons in Northumbria feared the king of Wessex might try to conquer them. These Northumbrians had got used to their new Viking rulers. Many people in Mercia were also unhappy. They did not like being ruled by a king of Wessex.

Source A

Bishop Eardwulf brought the bones of St Cuthbert to the Danes. Their king and army swore that there would be peace. They would support the monks.

This is from 'The History of St Cuthbert'. It tells how Anglo-Saxon monks helped the Viking kings of Northumbria. This was in the ninth century.

Source B

The Northumbrians welcomed the invaders. They gave in to them. This whole area of the country supported them.

William of Malmesbury wrote this. He told how Anglo-Saxons in Northumbria helped Viking invaders fight Athelstan. This was written in the twelfth century.

Source C

These are two silver pennies from York. The one below was made for Athelstan. It calls him 'King of all Britain'. On the right is one made for Olaf. He was a Viking ruler of York after Athelstan died.

How do we know?

Sources A and B show that some Anglo-Saxon people worked with the new Viking rulers. Some liked Viking rulers better than the kings from Wessex.

Source C shows Athelstan ruled over a lot of Britain. But after he died, Viking rulers came back to York.

King Athelstan

After Edward the Elder died, Athelstan became king of Wessex. In AD927 he invaded the Viking kingdom of Northumbria. He captured York.

Athelstan forced the kings of the Vikings, Welsh and Scots to accept him as the overlord of all Britain. In AD937 these enemies tried to kill him. They were helped by Anglo-Saxons from Northumbria, but Athelstan defeated them at the battle of Brunanburh. No one now is sure where this place was. In AD939 Athelstan died. Viking kings returned to York.

The Viking kings of York

Danish Vikings captured York in AD866. They called it Jorvik. The Danish Vikings became rulers of the kingdom of Northumbria.

In AD919, Norwegian Vikings captured York from the Danes. These Norwegian Vikings came from Dublin, in Ireland. For many years they ruled in York and in Dublin.

Vikings and the Anglo-Saxons

Anglo-Saxons in Northumbria soon got used to their Viking rulers. What mattered most to them was that Northumbria should be powerful. They were not bothered if their **king** was Danish or Norwegian. In AD927, Athelstan of Wessex took York. When he died, the Viking rulers returned to the city.

King Eric Bloodaxe

In AD947, a new Viking arrived in Northumbria. He was Eric Bloodaxe and he was the son of Harald Finehair, king of Norway. Eric was invited to become king of York. He ruled for one year, then he was driven out by Eadred, king of Wessex.

Source A

The son of Harald went with an army to England. And having conquered the island was betrayed and killed by the Northumbrians.

Adam of Bremen wrote this in about AD1075. The 'son of Harald' was Eric Bloodaxe. Adam lived in Germany.

Source B

From that time until now, Northumbria has been sad because it does not have its own king. And they miss the freedom they once had.

John of Wallingford writing about the death of Eric Bloodaxe. He wrote in the thirteenth century. This was 300 years after Eric died.

This tenth-century carving from York is a mixture of Viking and Anglo-Saxon art. In Eric's kingdom the Anglo-Saxon and Viking people usually worked together in peace.

How do we know?

Source B shows that many people in Northumbria were sad that Eric was killed. They liked having their own king. They did not mind that he was a Viking. Source C shows that in Northumbria many Anglo-Saxons and Vikings worked together in peace.

But Source A shows that some of these people plotted against Eric. They helped cause his death.

The return of Eric Bloodaxe

Four years later, in AD952, Eric returned. He was supported by the powerful people in Northumbria. But later they turned against him.

In AD954 Eric was killed in a battle. The people who killed him probably hoped to please the king of Wessex, who was getting more powerful. After Eric there were no more Viking kings of York.

The Vikings return

In AD980, Viking raiders attacked Anglo-Saxon England again. Over the next ten years, more and more attacks took place.

The new Viking raiders were Danish Vikings again. Towns like Southampton were attacked by these raiders. Most attacks were on the south coast towns of England. They stole treasure and valuable ornaments and books.

A new 'Great Army'

In AD991, a large Viking army sailed up the River Thames. These were Norwegian Vikings. They were led by Olaf Tryggvason. They fought a famous battle with the **Anglo-Saxon ealdorman** of Essex, who was called Byrhtnoth. This was the battle of Maldon. The Vikings won.

'Ethelred the Unready'

The Anglo-Saxon **king** in AD991 was Ethelred. He seemed unable to defeat the Vikings. His name meant 'royal wisdom'. Soon some people called him 'unraed', which meant 'no wisdom'. It sounds like the modern word 'unready', but it does not really mean this.

Source A

He dropped his yellow hilted sword to the ground,
He lacked the strength to hold the hard blade up.
Then the **heathens** cut him down,
And with him died those **warriors** who stood at his side.

This is from an Anglo-Saxon poem called 'The Battle of Maldon'. It tells how Byrhtnoth was killed by Viking raiders. It was probably written soon after the battle.

Source B

When the enemy was in the east, then our army was in the west. And when they were in the south, then our army was in the north.

From the Anglo-Saxon Chronicle, AD1010.

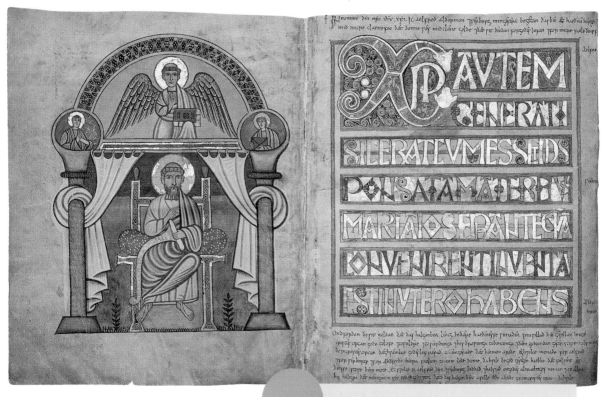

Source C

These two pages are from an expensive Christian book. It was stolen by Vikings from a church in Kent. It is not known when it was stolen. It was bought back by a man named Earl Alfred and his wife. Around the edge of the book the words tell how they bought it back. They did it, it says, because they loved God.

How do we know?

Source A tells us that Byrhtnoth was killed by Viking raiders. Source C shows the kinds of expensive things stolen by these raiders. These included beautiful books.

Source B shows why some people were unhappy at how Ethelred defended the country. They felt that the army was badly led. It was unable to stop the Vikings.

Danegeld

Ethelred agreed to give the Vikings money if they went away. In **Old English** this was called **Danegeld**. It cost a lot of money. In AD991 it cost £10,000. In AD994 it cost £16,000. These were huge amounts of money in the tenth century. Still the Vikings kept coming back. The attacks got worse.

The Viking conquest of England

After AD994, the Viking armies attacking England became larger and more powerful. They were led by Danish kings. These armies defeated the Anglo-Saxon warriors. The Viking kings became rulers of England.

The first **king** of Denmark to invade England was Swein Fork-Beard. He was helped by the Norwegian, Olaf Tryggvason.

The new Viking armies

The new Viking armies were different from those that had sailed to England in the past. The new ones were larger and they were more experienced. Swedish Vikings joined in for the first time. They came for the money paid to make them go away! In AD1002, **Danegeld** was £24,000. The Viking leaders shared it out among their army.

The massacre of the Danes

King Ethelred ordered the murder of every Danish person living in England. It is not known if his order was obeyed everywhere. No one knows how many died. These killings made Viking people abroad very angry and led to more Viking attacks. In AD1007, the Danegeld rose to £36,000. In AD1011, Vikings captured and killed the Archbishop of Canterbury.

Source A

Lions made from gold were seen on the ships. Dragons of different kinds breathed fire through their nostrils. There were glittering men of solid gold, or silver. They were almost as real as living people.

This is from a book called 'In Praise of Emma'. It was written soon after the attack by King Swein in AD1013. Emma had been the wife of King Ethelred. She was later made to marry King Cnut.

Source B

This stone is from Orkestad in Sweden. The inscription says 'Karsi and Gerbjorn had this stone put up in memory of Ulf their father. Ulf received Danegeld three times in England. The first was from Tosti. The second was from Thorkel. The third was from Cnut'. These were all Viking leaders.

The capture of England

In AD1013, the Danish king, Swein Fork-Beard, sailed to England again. He brought with him his son, Cnut. Swein was very rich, and he came with a huge army. They sailed in richly-carved warships. Ethelred fled from the country and Swein became king of England, but he died in AD1014. Cnut went back to Denmark, but he came back again the next year.

There was more fighting across England. In AD1016, Ethelred died. By the end of the year, Cnut had become king of all England. The Vikings had captured the whole country.

How do we know?

Source A shows that Swein Fork-Beard must have been rich to have ships like this one. But the writer might have made him sound rich to impress people.

Source B shows Swedish Vikings joined the new attacks to get Danegeld.

The end of the Viking Age

In AD1066, Anglo-Saxon England was invaded again by a Viking army. Shortly afterwards, the last of the Anglo-Saxon kings was killed by the Normans.

The Danish **king**, Cnut, became ruler of England in AD1016. He died in AD1035. For a short time England was ruled by his sons. Vikings and **Anglo-Saxons** mixed and married. After the deaths of Cnut's sons, the new Anglo-Saxon kings continued to use Viking **warriors** as their bodyguards.

In AD1042, England was ruled by an Anglo-Saxon king again. This was Edward the Confessor. He was the son of Ethelred the Unready. He had lived in Normandy, in France, while Viking kings ruled England. When he came back to England he brought many of his **Norman** friends with him.

The death of King Edward

King Edward died in January 1066. Who was now going to be king? An Anglo-Saxon named Harold Godwinson, Earl of Wessex, became king, but there were others who thought they should be king of England.

Source A

Earl Tostig and the king talked a lot together. At last they decided to invade England that summer.

This is from King Harald's Saga. It tells how Tostig and Harald Hardrada planned to invade England. It was written in the thirteenth century.

Source B

The bodyguards of King Harold Godwinson at the battle of Hastings. They were armed with axes and fought like Vikings. They were called 'housecarls'.

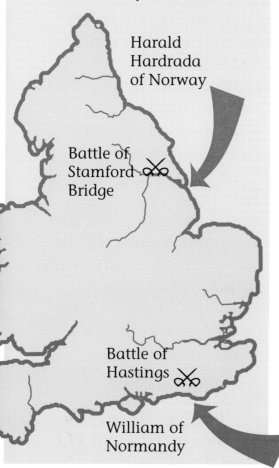

The invasions of Harald Hardrada and William of Normandy in 1066.

Harald Hardrada of Norway

Battle of Stamford Bridge

Battle of Hastings

William of Normandy

How do we know?

Source A tells us that Harold Godwinson's brother, Tostig, helped the enemy of the English king.

Source B shows how Viking ideas caught on in England. The bodyguards of the Anglo-Saxon king fought like Vikings.

William and Harald Hardrada

Duke William of Normandy said Edward had promised that he should be king. His family were descended from Vikings, who had been given land in France. Normandy means 'land of the north-men'. In Norway lived King Harald Hardrada. He claimed that he should be king of England too.

Stamford Bridge and Hastings

In September 1066, Harald Hardrada landed in the north of England. He was helped by Tostig, King Harold Godwinson's brother. Tostig betrayed his own brother. Hardrada and Tostig were killed at the battle of Stamford Bridge, by King Harold Godwinson.

That same month, Duke William landed in the south of England. He killed King Harold at the battle of Hastings.

The end of the Viking age

In AD1069 and 1075, more Viking armies attacked England but were defeated. These were the last Viking invasions of England. The Viking age was over.

Glossary

Anglo-Saxons people living in England when the Vikings invaded

armour metal worn to protect a warrior from harm

bishop an important leader in the Christian Church

border where two kingdoms meet; the edge of the land ruled by a king

burh a fort, or a defended town. They were built by Anglo-Saxon rulers against Viking attacks.

chainmail rings of metal fixed together to make a coat. It was used to protect warriors.

Danegeld money paid by Anglo-Saxon rulers to make Vikings go away

ealdorman an important Anglo-Saxon. A person who looked after part of the country for the ruler.

heathen a person who is not a Christian. Someone who worshipped the Viking gods.

host a Viking army

king the ruler of a kingdom. The Viking invaders of England and the Anglo-Saxons were ruled by a number of different kings.

Latin the language used by the church and well-educated people in Anglo-Saxon England

mancus (mancuses) an amount of money worth 30 pennies. In the ninth century it would buy a cow.

manor an area of land around a manor house or important farm

monastery a place where monks or nuns live

Norman a person from Normandy in France. The first Normans were Viking settlers. The name means 'north-men'.

Old English the language spoken by the Anglo-Saxons

pagan a person who is not a Christian. Someone who worshipped the Viking gods.

raft things tied together to make a floating island

reeve an important servant of an Anglo-Saxon ruler

thegn an important warrior who fought for an Anglo-Saxon ruler

trade buying and selling things

translate change words from one language to another one

treaty an agreement written down

warriors soldiers who fought for their lord or king. They were rewarded with gold and silver and lived with their lord. Some warriors went on to become important lords themselves.

wedge a triangle shape

Timeline – Romans, Anglo-Saxons and Vikings

AD1

AD100

AD200

AD300

AD400

AD500

AD600

AD700

AD800

Viking Age

AD900

AD1000

AD1100

AD700

AD800

AD900

AD1000

AD1100

AD789	First Viking attacks on Britain
AD793	Vikings attack Lindisfarne
AD850	Vikings first spend winter in England
All Anglo-Saxon kingdoms are defeated by Vikings, except for Wessex
AD886	Alfred and Guthrum agree a peace treaty
AD937	Battle of Brunanburh
AD947	Eric Bloodaxe becomes King of York
AD980	New Viking attacks on England
AD1013	Viking King Swein conquers England
AD1042	End of Viking rule in England
AD1075	Last Viking invasion of England

Index

Numbers in plain type (4) refer to the text.
Numbers in italic type (4) refer to a caption.